INTRODUCTION

"This sounds really cool, but what do I play on it?"

This is often the first comment someone makes after playing a harmonic minor tuned harmonica for the first time. It's relatively easy to vamp a few chords that sound like a tango, or perhaps play an approximation of something from the musical "Fiddler On The Roof", but most harmonica players do not have a readily available repertoire for the harmonic minor tuning.

For reasons that will be made clear in the following pages, there are not many familiar Western melodies that utilise the harmonic minor scale exclusively. However, there are a few, as well as the countless tunes from other cultures that are based on the harmonic minor. This book gathers together one hundred and one of them, all arranged for a harmonic minor harp in Am and presented in both standard notation and tablature. (For more details regarding the tablature, please refer to page 116). As far as I know, this is the first published collection of tunes specifically for the harmonic minor harmonica.

This book concentrates mostly on traditional tunes in the public domain, but there are a few examples of 20th century popular tunes that are based on the harmonic minor scale, for example "Istanbul (Not Constantinople)" (a hit for The Four Lads in the early 1950s and a hit for They Might Be Giants almost forty years later), "Anniversary Song" (made famous by Al Jolson in the 1940s, but based on an earlier tune called "Waves of the Danube", by Romanian composer Ion Ivanovici), tangos such as "La Cumparsita" and "Hernando's Hideaway", Billie Holiday's "Strange Fruit", "Bei Mir Bist Du Schoen" (well known to many US Midwesterners from root beer commercials in the 1970s) and others. After working through the pieces in this book, these tunes should be easy enough to figure out for yourself.

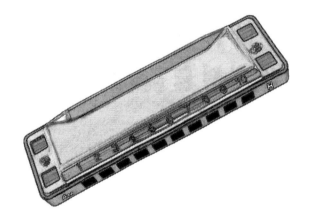

THE

HARMONIC MINOR

TUNEBOOK

ONE HUNDRED AND ONE TUNES
FOR THE TEN HOLE HARMONICA
IN HARMONIC MINOR TUNING

BY

PAT MISSIN

www.patmissin.com

THE HARMONIC MINOR TUNEBOOK:
One Hundred and One Tunes for the Ten Hole Harmonica in Harmonic
Minor Tuning

Printed in the United States of America

First printing 2012

ISBN-10: 1479133140

ISBN-13: 978-1479133147

www.createspace.com

CONTENTS

ABOUT THE HARMONIC MINOR SCALE

Before getting into harmonica-specific information, a very brief discussion of relevant music theory may be in order. This is not absolutely required in order to play the tunes in this book, so feel free to come back to this stuff later, or even to skip it entirely.

MAJOR AND MINOR SCALES AND MODES

A scale is a sequence of notes, in either ascending or descending order. The most familiar example is the diatonic major scale, the well-known Do, Re, Mi, Fa, So, La, Ti, Do of solfège. The white notes of the piano keyboard give this scale in the key of C major - C D E F G A B C - and this is the scale you get if you play the notes between hole 4 blow and hole 7 blow on a C major diatonic harmonica.

As a harmonica player, you may also know that a scale can be rearranged into different *modes*. If you play your C harmonica in second position, or cross harp style, assuming you are not bending to produce notes outside of the scale, then you will be playing the G mixolydian mode. Third position on a C major harp gives the dorian mode in D. Fourth position on a C harp gives the aeolian mode in A. The aeolian mode is also known as the natural minor scale, the term "natural" being used because is it drawn from the parent C major scale without adding any sharps or flats, giving the sequence A B C D E F G A.

The aeolian mode or natural minor is very commonly found in folk music and early Western art music, familiar examples of tunes in this mode are "God Rest Ye Merry Gentlemen", "Black is the Colour of My True Love's Hair", "When Johnny Comes Marching Home" and more recent songs such as Van Morrison's "Moondance" and "The Sound of Silence" by Simon and Garfunkel.

THE HARMONIC MINOR SCALE

As its name suggests, the harmonic minor scale comes into play when we are dealing with the harmony of a minor key tune. In the Western tradition, chords are derived by combining various notes from the scale to which they are to serve as accompaniment. You may be familiar with the so-called "three chord trick", where learning just three basic chords allows you to strum a guitar accompaniment to literally thousands of blues, country, rock and pop songs. These three chords are the tonic, the subdominant and the dominant chords and in the key of C major would be C major (comprising the notes C, E and G), F major (comprising the notes F, A and C) and G7 (comprising the notes G, B, D and F). These are commonly known as the I, IV and V chords because they are built on the first, fourth and fifth notes of the scale.

Here is a diagram showing how these chords are derived:

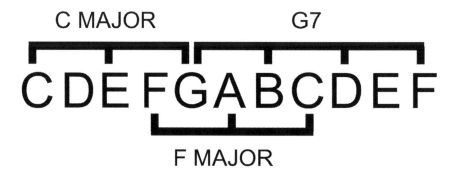

If this same process is applied to the natural minor scale, the chords A minor (comprising the notes A C E), D minor (comprising the notes D F and A) and Em7 (comprising the notes E G B and D) are obtained:

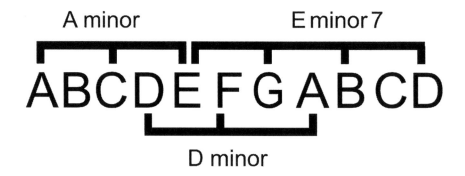

However, the general consensus of the great musical minds of the day was that whereas the chord rooted on the fifth note of the major scale tended to want to resolve to the tonic chord, the chord rooted on the fifth note of the natural scale did not provide a strong enough sense of tension to do this, making the natural minor a tonally weak scale. The solution to this was to sharpen the seventh note of the scale. In our A minor scale the note G is raised to G# and gives the chords A minor, D minor and E7 (comprising the notes E G# B and D):

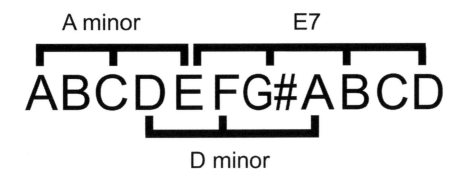

The E7 chord has a feeling of tension that wants to resolve to the Am chord, helping to strengthen the tonality of the scale. Changing the G natural to a G# also means that other chords can be derived from this scale that are not naturally present in the major or natural minor scale. For this reason, the scale was termed the *harmonic* minor scale, as its main purpose in Western art music was the provide the raw materials for the harmonic structure of passages in minor keys.

THE MELODIC MINOR SCALE

However, the raising of the seventh note of the scale introduces problems as well. The distance between the sixth and seventh notes of the harmonic minor (F and G#) is an augmented second - something that was not considered a nice neat melodic step in Western art music at the time - in fact it is the feature that gives the harmonic minor its exotic sound to Western ears. To remedy this, another minor scale was brought into use. There had often been a tendency amongst singers and string players to sharpen certain notes in ascent and flatten them slightly in descent, often referred to as "expressive intonation", so to smooth out that augmented second of the harmonic minor scale, both the sixth and seventh notes of the natural minor were sharpened in ascent, then made natural again on the way back down, making a nice neat sequence of wholetone and semitone intervals. As this was intended to be used for melodies, it was termed the *melodic* minor scale and in the key of Am it looks like this:

A B C D E F# G# A G F E D C B A

Of course, in the real world musicians do not adhere quite so strictly to these theoretical constructions, so minor melodies often freely mix the natural, melodic and harmonic minor scales. However, this brief overview will have helped explain why it can be tricky to find familiar melodies that neatly fit the harmonic minor harmonica

In other parts of the world, musicians did not have such a problem with augmented second intervals in melodies, especially in those cultures where melodies were accompanied by drones, rather than chord sequences. East European, Middle Eastern and Asian musicians were quite happy to use the harmonic minor scale as a melodic structure. Also, there are a few Western tunes in minor keys that have chordally derived melodies that are playable on the harmonic minor harp, so finding the 101 tunes for this book was a bit of a challenge, but not an impossible task.

ABOUT THE HARMONIC MINOR HARMONICA

Although alternate tunings for the diatonic harmonicas are generally perceived as being relatively new, harmonic minor harps have been around for some time. They first appeared in dealers' catalogs in the late 1800s and started appearing on recordings in the late 1920s. Hohner's Orchester model was probably been the most popular harmonic minor 10-hole harp until it was discontinued in the early 1980s. Lee Oskar picked up the slack a few years later and made his signature diatonic model available in a harmonic minor version in all 12 keys.

Currently, 10-hole harmonicas in harmonic minor tuning are available from Tombo, Lee Oskar, Hohner, Suzuki and Seydel - the latter have also made them for other companies such as Bushman. Suzuki also make a 5-hole miniature harmonica in harmonic minor, tuned like holes 4 to 8 of the 10-hole version.

LAYOUT OF THE HARMONIC MINOR HARMONICA

The harmonic minor tuning is laid out with the same general idea as the standard major diatonic. Holes 4 to 7 provide a complete scale and the upper and lower octaves have gaps and/or repeated notes. Here is a diagram showing the layout - blow notes above, draw notes below:

	A	C	E	A	C	E	A	C	E	A	
Am	1	2	3	4	5	6	7	8	9	10	H
	B	E	G#	B	D	F	G#	B	D	F	

With a major tuned harmonica, blowing produces the tonic chord and drawing produces the dominant chord. This is also true of the harmonic minor - blowing a few holes anywhere on a harmonic minor harp in Am produces an Am chord; drawing in the lower five holes produces an E7 chord and if you include a few higher draw notes, you'll be playing E7♭9 (E dominant seventh flat ninth).

If you compare a harmonic minor harp with a major diatonic harp rooted on the same key note (such as AmH and A major), you will see that only a few notes are different - on the harmonic minor, blow 2, 5 and 8 and draw 6 and 9 are all lowered by one semitone.

AVAILABLE BENDS ON THE HARMONIC MINOR

The bent notes that are available on a harmonica depend on the pitches of the blow and draw reeds that share each chamber. In each hole of the 10-hole harmonica, the higher note can be bent down to a pitch about a semitone above the lower note in that hole. Here are the available bent notes of the harmonic minor harp in Am.

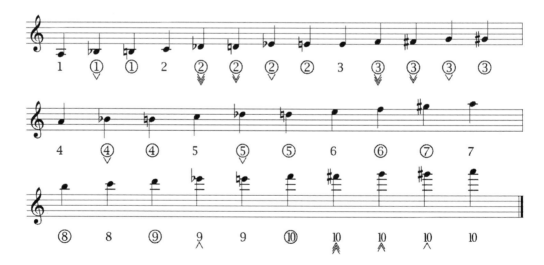

Each of the different keys of the harmonic minor has the same bends available, although obviously they produce different pitches. Certain bends might be rather tricky in certain keys, especially all those blow bends in hole 10.

MAJOR DIATONIC VS HARMONIC MINOR

It is, of course, perfectly possible to play in minor keys on a major diatonic harmonica, including playing the harmonic minor scale. In a few cases, this might even be the best way to play a harmonic minor based tune, but most of the time the harmonic minor harp will have the advantage. Here is an A harmonic minor scale played in the midrange of a C major diatonic:

As you can see, a couple of bends are required. The hole 3 bend is especially important to get right, as it is your key note. Things are made even more difficult if the tune requires the low seventh of the scale (G# in the key of Am), as in this example:

Notice how hard it is to get good clear separation of the G# and the A, not to mention keeping them in tune and playing them with good tone. Now here is that same phrase on an A harmonic minor harp:

Notice how this phrase flows much more smoothly on this tuning and with much less effort on the part of the player. Plus with the harmonic minor, you can harmonise the scale by playing a couple of holes at a time, or use tongue-blocked chords to support the melody and so on.

PLAYING THE HARMONIC MINOR IN OTHER POSITIONS

Like the major diatonic harmonica, the harmonic minor was designed to be played in what harmonica players call first position - i.e., using an AmH harmonica to play in a tune in the key of Am. However, also like the major diatonic, the harmonic minor can be played in numerous other positions. As you may already know, in harmonica terminology the term *position* refers to the tonal centre of the tune relative to the key of the harmonica used to play it. If you were to use a C harp to play in the key of C, that would be first position, also commonly called straight harp style. If, as is the case with the majority of blues and rock harmonica playing, you were to use your C harmonica to play a tune in the key of G, that would be second position, also known as cross harp. If you were to use a D harp to play a tune in A, or an A harp to play a tune in E, that would also be second position. In theory, there are 12 possible positions on each harp, but most players only use a few of them. This sort of approach can be very useful for instruments like the harmonica, which are typically available tuned to several different keys. As the harmonic minor is something of a specialist scale in the first place, use of the different positions is going to be even more limited than with the standard major diatonic tuning. However, this book contains tunes in at least three different positions of the harmonic minor harp.

MODES OF THE HARMONIC MINOR SCALE

If you play the basic scale of the major diatonic harmonica without using any bends, the different positions each produce what is termed a *mode* of the major scale. The first mode of the major scale is called the ionian and it is just the plain vanilla major scale you get when you play in first position. The second mode is called the dorian mode and that's what you get when you play your harmonica in third position, i.e. using a C harp to play against a tonal centre of D. The third mode is called phrygian and that's what you get playing in fifth position with no bends, i.e. using your C harp to play against a tonal centre of E. There are seven such modes in total, one for each note of the major scale. (If any of this is completely new to you, I recommend picking up a good harmonica book to help brush up on some basics - Winslow Yerxa's "Harmonicas for Dummies" is a particularly good one.)

14

The harmonic minor scale also has seven modes, although their names are not universally standardised. The first mode is, of course, the harmonic minor scale:

This is known in Arabic music as *nahawand-hijaz*, in Turkish music as *buselik-hicaz* and it is the basis of the Indian raga *kirvani*.

The second mode is played in third position (key of B on an AmH harp):

This mode is rarely used and doesn't have any common names, although I have heard it called *pseudo-Turkish*.

The third mode of the harmonic minor is played in tenth position (C on an AmH harmonica):

Another rarely used mode, this is a major scale with an augmented fifth.

The fourth mode is played in twelfth position (D on an AmH):

This scale is commonly known as Romanian minor and is called *hemavati* in Indian music, *nikriz* in Arabic music, *souzinak* in Greek music and *misheberekh* in Jewish music and klezmer.

The fifth mode of the harmonic minor is played in second position (E on an AmH):

This scale is commonly called phrygian dominant and is known as *ahava rabba* or *freygish* in Jewish music and klezmer, *hijaz-nahawand* in Arabic music, *humayun* in Persian music, *hitzaz* in Greek music, *vakulabharanam* in Indian music, as well as by many other names.

The sixth mode of the harmonic minor is played in ninth position (F on an AmH harp):

This is often called lydian #2 by jazz musicians, this is the *kosalam* scale of Indian music theory.

Finally, the seventh mode is played in sixth position (G# on an AmH harp):

Another rarely used mode, I have heard this one called *ultralocrian*.

All the above examples are shown in the middle octave, where they can all be played without bends. Obviously, with a few bends here and there, they can be transposed to the upper or lower octaves.

OTHER SCALES

In addition to the modes that are built into the harmonic minor scale, with a few bends there are several other scales that lie quite well in this tuning. The melodic minor scale (described in the previous chapter) is quite playable in the lowest octave of the harmonic minor tuning:

Notice that this scale requires a bend on hole 3 draw on the way up and two different bends in the same hole on the way down. It can be challenging to play all theses bends perfectly, especially that three semitone bend. A good exercise for working on your intonation with this scale is the opening section of J. S. Bach's well known "Bourrée in Em", here transposed to A minor:

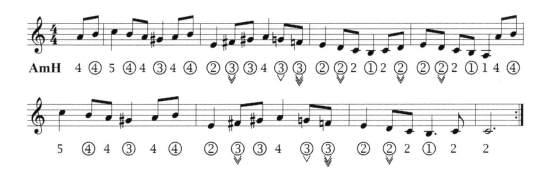

The ascending form of the melodic minor is often used as a scale in its own right. Its common name of jazz minor gives a hint as to its popularity with jazz musicians, but it is also found in tunes associated with the Swedish bagpipes, of which there are a few examples in this book.

Another scale that lies nicely in the lower octave is the so-called double harmonic minor, also referred to as the Hungarian minor scale, Gypsy minor and other names, including *nawa-athar* in Arabic music and *niavent* in Greek music. It is essentially a harmonic minor scale with the fourth degree raised:

It is also playable in the middle octave with an overblow on hole 5 and in the upper octave with single semitone blow bends on holes 9 and 10.

A related scale, actually the fifth mode of the Hungarian minor, is often called the Gypsy major scale and is the *bhairav* scale of Indian music, *hitzazkiar* in Greek music and *hijaz-kar* in Arabic music theory.

This is most well-known to Western ears from the tune "Misirlou". It can also be played an octave lower with the use of an overblow in hole 5.

The fifth mode of the ascending melodic minor scale is commonly (and rather vaguely) called the Hindu scale. In Indian music it is the scale *charukesi*:

This scale could be thought of as being the lower half of a major scale combined with the upper half of the natural minor scale, which gives it a very distinctive flavour. It is commonly used in Hindi film music and I am told that Led Zeppelin made extensive use of it in such tunes as "Ten Years Gone".

18

Although the aforementioned scales lie especially well on the harmonic minor harp, in theory any scale can be played in the lower range of this tuning. The harmonic minor layout gives you almost one and a half octaves of chromatic scale without having to use overblows:

In practice, this may be easier said than done, of course. However, if you need to play a highly chromatic passage without resorting to a chromatic harmonica, it is worth trying it in the lower half of the harmonic minor harp.

ABOUT THE TUNES

The tunes in this collection are taken from a wide variety of sources - early Western composers, klezmer, the folk musics of the British Isles, Europe, Scandinavia, the Balkan countries, the Middle East and beyond. Included are sea shanties, waltzes, bourrées, freilachs, schottisches, gavottes, Christmas carols, hymns and much more.

The tunes are divided into two sections - those that can be played without note bending and those that require some bends. I have arranged the tunes in the range of the harmonica where I think they sound best. Many of the tunes without bends could be played in a different octave of the harmonica by using a few bent notes.

As with the standard major tuning, 2 draw and 3 blow on the harmonic minor tuning produce the same notes. In the tablature I have suggested whichever one I feel makes the most sense for the tune, but feel free to disagree with my choice and play the one that works best for you.

The difficulty level ranges from extremely easy to moderately challenging, but with the exception of a few very easy tunes at the start of the chapter, they are presented in no particular order. I have arranged all the tunes for a harmonic minor harp in Am. I did this for a couple of reasons, the main one being that most harmonica players are unlikely to have a set of harmonic minor harps in all keys. However, some of the tunes were originally written in a different key and many of them might sound better on a higher or lower pitched harp. If you have other harmonic minor harps available to you, feel free to experiment and choose whichever key you think best suits the tune. Obviously, the tablature will work fine with a harmonic minor harp in any key - the music will simply come out at a higher or lower pitch than shown in the notation.

.mp3 files of all the tunes are available for free download from my web site:

www.patmissin.com/downloads.html

TUNES WITHOUT BENDS

AH, POOR BIRD

England

EGYPT

James Leach

A couple of nice easy tunes to start out. "Ah Poor Bird" possibly dates back as far as Elizabethan times and is often sung as a round.

"Egypt" is a hymn tune composed by British-born hand-loom weaver and self-taught musician James Leach (1762-1798), with lyrics written by Charles Wesley.

ROBIN HOOD AND THE STRANGER

England

AmH   4   ④5   ④5   ⑤   5   ④4   ③   3   4   ④5   ⑤   ④   5   ⑤ 6

       6   5   ⑤   ④   5   ④4   ③   5   ④   4   ③ 4 ④   4

THE BAILIFF'S DAUGHTER OF ISLINGTON

England

AmH   5   ④5   ④   5   ④   6   4   ③   ②   5   5   ⑤6 ⑥6 ⑤   6   5

       5   ④5   ⑤   5   ④   6   4   ③   4   ④5   ③   ②   4   ④ 5   4

Two beautiful folk songs from England, dating back to the 17th and 18th centuries respectively.

ES SAß EIN KLEIN WILD VÖGELEIN

Germany

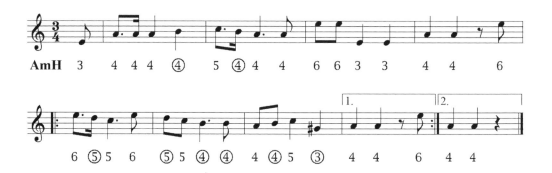

¿ONDE VAS POR AGUA?

Spain (Asturias)

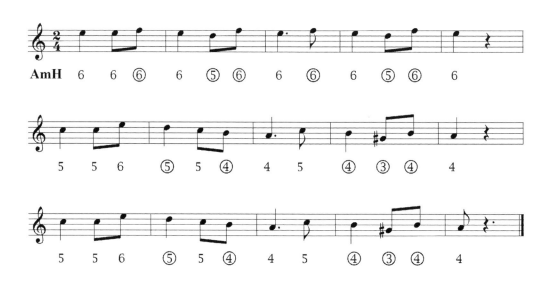

Two European folk songs, whose titles translate as "There Sits a Little Wild Bird" and "Where Do You Go For Water?"

TAFTA HINDI

Egypt

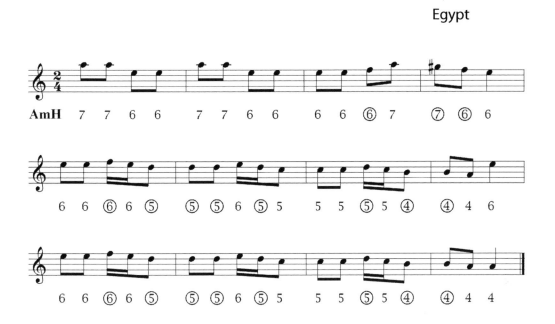

AmH   7   7   6   6   7   7   6   6   6   6   ⑥   7   ⑦   ⑥   6

6   6   ⑥   6   ⑤   ⑤   ⑤   6   ⑤   5   5   5   ⑤   5   ④   ④   4   6

6   6   ⑥   6   ⑤   ⑤   ⑤   6   ⑤   5   5   5   ⑤   5   ④   ④   4   4

NOR A MAME

David Einhorn

AmH   3   5   ③   4   3   5   ③   4   3   5   ④   ④   ③   ②   4

5   ⑤   6   6   ④   5   ⑤   ⑤   4   ④   5   5   ④   ③   ②   4   5   ④   ③   ②   6   4

Two more relatively simple tunes. "Tafta Hindi" means "Indian Tafeta" and has its origins in the calls of marketplace vendors. Syncopated versions are often played for belly dancers. "Nor A Mame" ("Only A Mother") is a Yiddish lullaby written in 1917, although the tune is probably much older.

NOUS ETIONS TROIS BERGERETTES

France

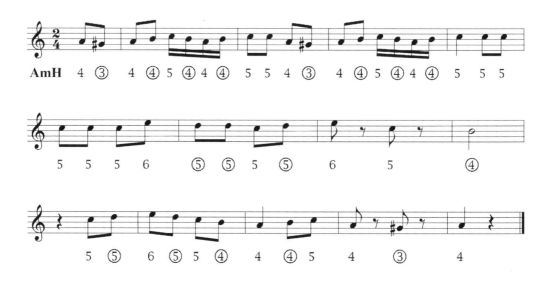

HOY ES LA GRAN NOCHE DE LOS SANTOS REYES

Spain (Asturias)

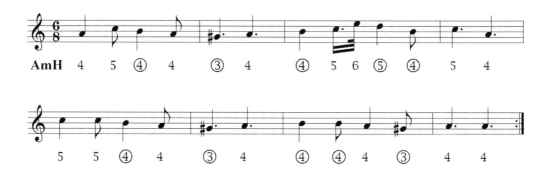

Two traditional Christmas carols from Europe. The first title translates as "We Were Three Young Shepherdesses", the second as "Tonight is the Night of the Three Kings"

THE OLD WAITS CAROL

England

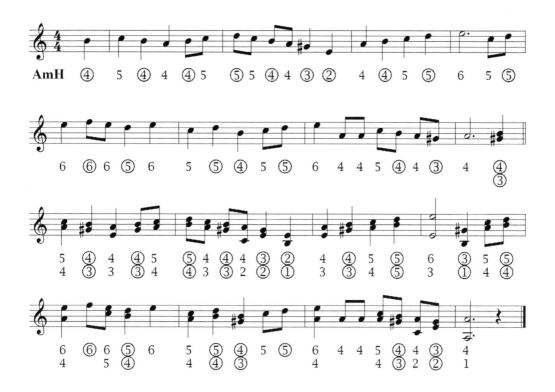

AmH ④ 5 ④ 4 ④ 5 ⑤ 5 ④ 4 ③ ② 4 ④ 5 ⑤ 6 5 ⑤

6 ⑥ 6 ⑤ 6 5 ⑤ ④ 5 ⑤ 6 4 4 5 ④ 4 ③ 4 ④
                                                                ③

5 ④ 4 ④ 5 ⑤ 4 ④ 4 ③ ② 4 ④ 5 ⑤ 6 ③ 5 ⑤
4 ③ 3 ③ 4 ④ 3 ③ 2 ② ① 3 ③ 4 ⑤ 3 ① 4 ④

6 ⑥ 6 ⑤ 6 5 ⑤ ④ 5 ⑤ 6 4 4 5 ④ 4 ③ 4
4   5 ④   4 ④ ③   4   4 ③ 2 ② 1

Another traditional Christmas tune, also known as "The Bellman's Song" and "The Moon Shines Bright". In this arrangement, the melody is played the first time through as a single note line, then played with a harmony the second time. Most of the harmonies simply use adjacent holes on the harmonica, but there are a couple of bits that require tongue-blocked intervals. If these give you trouble, just play the highest note and it should still sound OK.

AH, LITTLE DUCK OF THE MEADOWS

Russia

Another harmonized tune, this time using full chords as well as double stops

SIRDES

Armenia

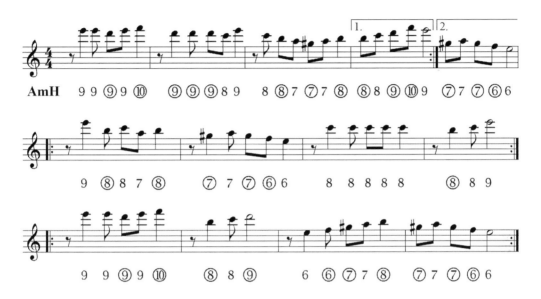

AmH 9 9 ⑨ 9 ⑩   ⑨ ⑨ ⑨ 8 9   8 ⑧ 7 ⑦ 7 ⑧   ⑧ 8 ⑨ ⑩ 9   ⑦ 7 ⑦ ⑥ 6

9 ⑧ 8 7 ⑧   ⑦ 7 ⑦ ⑥ 6   8 8 8 8   ⑧ 8 9

9 9 ⑨ 9 ⑩   ⑧ 8 ⑨   6 ⑥ ⑦ 7 ⑧   ⑦ 7 ⑦ ⑥ 6

IGRALE SE DELIJE

Serbia

AmH ⑨ ⑨ ⑨ 8   ⑧ 7 7   ⑤ ⑥ 7 7   ⑦ ⑥ ⑤

⑤ ⑥ 7   ⑧ 7 7   ⑦ ⑥ 6 ⑤   6 6 6

A pair of tunes to introduce two of the other modes of the harmonic minor scale. "Sirdes" uses the fifth mode, played in second position on the harmonic minor harp (6 blow and 9 blow as the keynote). "Igrale Se Delije" uses the fourth mode, played in twelfth position (5 draw and 9 draw as the keynote).

DOL-LI-LA

England

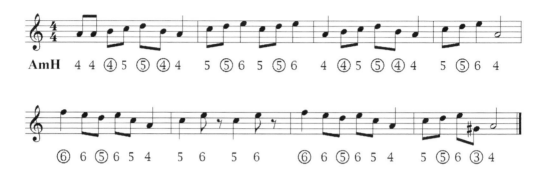

SAITH NOS OLAU

Wales

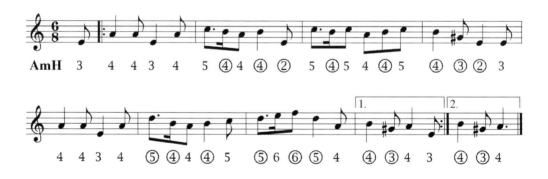

Back to the British Isles again with a dance tune from Northumbria and a jig from Wales whose title translates as "Seven Light Nights"

ROSLIN CASTLE

Scotland

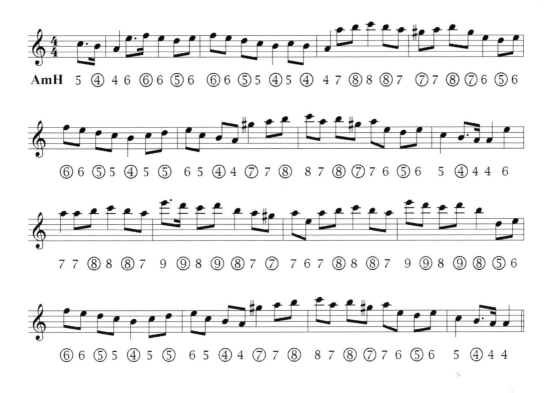

Roslin Castle is in Midlothian, Scotland and was built some time in the 14th century. This tune has also been used as the melody for several different sets of lyrics, including "The Gloomy Night is Gathering Fast", by Robbie Burns.

HAVA NAGILA

Israel

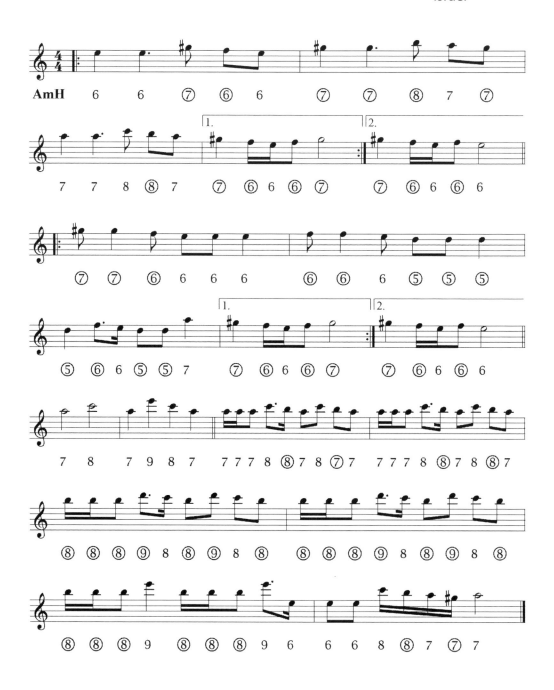

Probably the most well-known piece of music from the Hebrew tradition, the title means "Let Us Rejoice".

"Zemer Atik", also known as "Nigun Atik", is another popular dance tune from this tradition.

ZEMER ATIK

Israel

GRIM KING OF THE GHOSTS

England

Dating back to the early 18th century and also known as "The Lunatick Lover", this is another tune that has been used as the melody to several different sets of lyrics, including "The Father's Wholesome Admonition", "The Protestant's Joy," "Colin's Complaint", and "Hail to the Myrtle Shades,"

AZIZ JOON

Iran

A Mazandarani folk song from Northern Iran, whose title means "Sweetheart".
6/8 time signatures are extremely common in Iranian and Persian music, but
they have a completely different feel to the 6/8 jigs of the British and European folk dance traditions.

SPARVENS POLSKA

Sweden

A tune from Södermanland on the Baltic coast of Southwest Sweden. The title is often translated as "Sparrow's Polka", but the polska is not a polka. Polska (also called *polsk* or *pols*, depending on the region) is a dance form from Sweden, Norway, Finland and Denmark in 3/4 or 9/8, whereas polkas are usually in 2/4 time.

OLSON'S POLSKA

Sweden

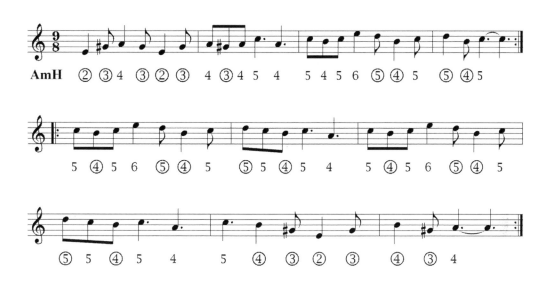

POLSKA FROM JÄMTLAND

Sweden

HAIDA HAIDA

Israel

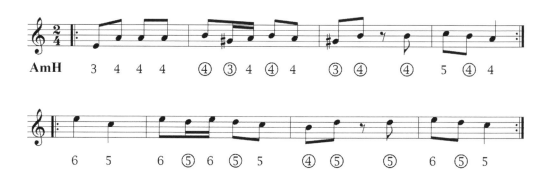

AmH 3 4 4 4 ④ ③ 4 ④ 4 ③ ④ ④ 5 ④ 4

6 5 6 ⑤ 6 ⑤ 5 ④ ⑤ ⑤ 6 ⑤ 5

MECHOL HA SHNAYIM

Israel

AmH ⑨ ⑨ ⑨ 8 ⑧ 7 9 ⑩ 9 ⑨ 8 ⑧ 7 ⑧ 8 ⑨ 8 ⑧ 8 ⑨ 9 9 ⑩ 9

6 ⑥ ⑦ 7 ⑧ ⑦ 7 ⑧ 8 ⑧ 7 6 ⑥ ⑦ 7 ⑧ ⑦ 7 ⑧ 7

⑨ ⑨ ⑨ 8 ⑧ 7 9 ⑩ 9 ⑨ 8 ⑧ 7 ⑧ 8 ⑨ 8 ⑧ 8 ⑨ 9 9 ⑩ 9

Two traditional Jewish dance tunes. The first tune also has lyrics, consisting of the words "haida haida" repeated over and over again.

38

YOIMACHIGUSA

Tadasuke Ono

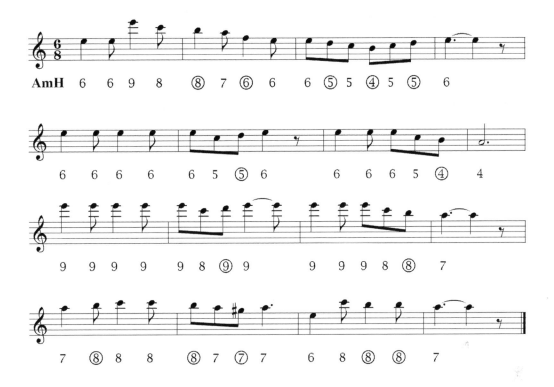

The title of this popular Japanese song means "Evening Primrose". The lyrics were written by painter and poet Takehisa Yumeji (1884-1934) in 1913 and set to music a few years later by Tadasuke Ono (1895-1929)

POLKA

Belgium

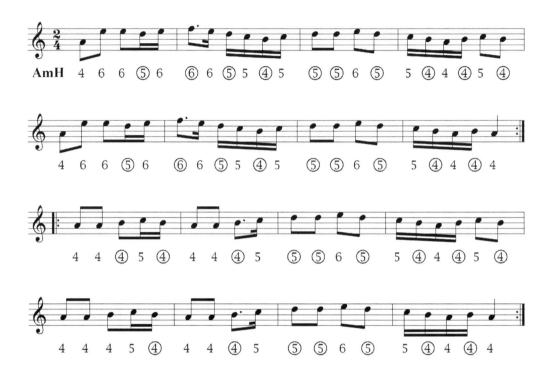

AmH 4 6 6 ⑤ 6   ⑥ 6 ⑤ 5 ④ 5   ⑤ ⑤ 6 ⑤   5 ④ 4 ④ 5 ④

4 6 6 ⑤ 6   ⑥ 6 ⑤ 5 ④ 5   ⑤ ⑤ 6 ⑤   5 ④ 4 ④ 4

4 4 ④ 5 ④   4 4 ④ 5   ⑤ ⑤ 6 ⑤   5 ④ 4 ④ 5 ④

4 4 4 5 ④   4 4 ④ 5   ⑤ ⑤ 6 ⑤   5 ④ 4 ④ 4

A pair of untitled polkas. The polka originated in Central Europe in the early 19th century and quickly became immensely popular worldwide. More than a century before "Beatlemania" swept the world, the British satirical magazine *Punch* featured an article on "that obstinate and tormenting disease, the Polkamania" in an issue from 1845, stating that "no cure has as yet been proposed for Polkamania".

POLKKA

Finland

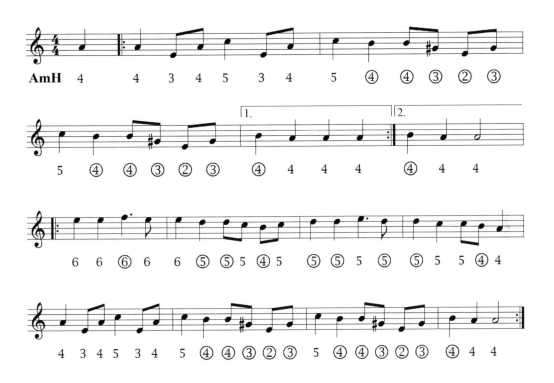

41

MR. LANE'S MAGGOT

England

I don't know who Mr. Lane was, but the maggot was a dance craze that was sweeping the nation back in the 17th century. The tune is also known as "Richmond Ball" and "Stanley For Ever" and has had various sets of lyrics attached to it.

SIRBA DE CIMPOI

Romania

A dance tune traditionally played on the Romanian bagpipes. It does not feature the raised seventh degree of the harmonic minor scale, so it could be played on a harmonica in natural minor tuning, or even in 4th position on a standard major harp. However, I think it sounds best on the harmonic minor harmonica.

GAVOTTE

France

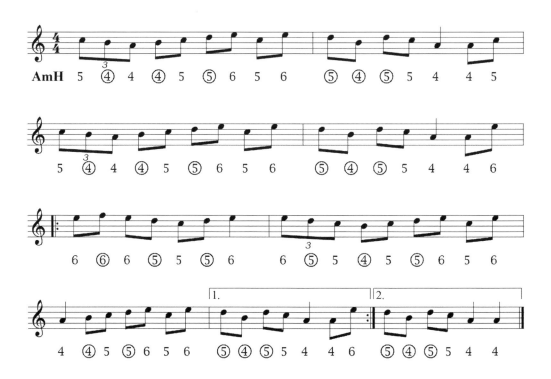

The gavotte is a folk dance that originated in France in the late 17th century. It later became very popular with baroque composers, including Johann Sebastian Bach.

The first tune is another that does not use the raised seventh degree of the harmonic minor scale, but again, I think that it sounds best played on a harmonic minor harp.

44

GAVOTTE

France

MR. TURVEYDROP

England(?)

I don't know anything about this rather nice tune, other than Mr. Turveydrop being a character in "Bleak House", by Charles Dickens.

LÅNGDANS FRÅN SOLLERON

Sweden

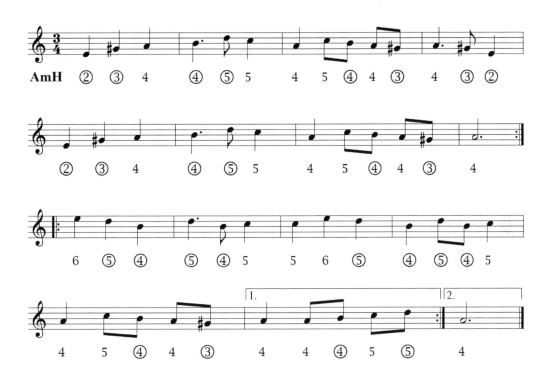

A traditional Long Dance from Solleron, in central Sweden. The Long Dance form is said to date from as far back as the early Renaissance.

ORIENTALISHE MELODIE

Klezmer

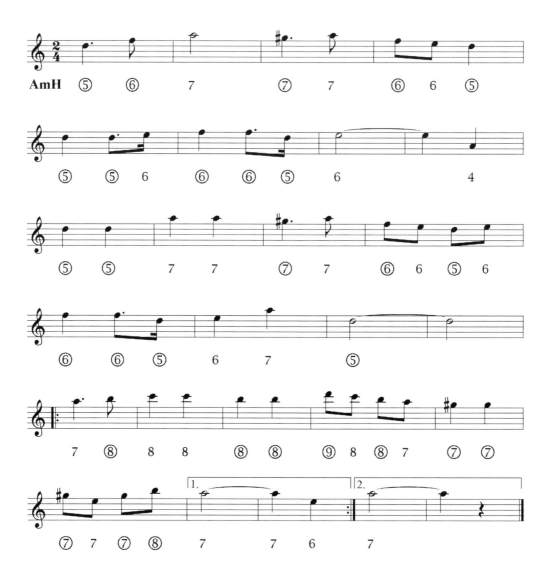

I don't know the title of this haunting piece set in the fourth mode of the harmonic minor scale (5 draw as your tonic note), but a highly ornamented version of it was played by Klezmer violinist Max Leibowitz as part of his medley "Orientalishe Melodien", recorded on an Emerson 78 way back in 1919.

PEERIE WEE FREILACHS

Klezmer

Another tune from the klezmer tradition, this time a dance tune in the fifth mode of the harmonic minor, played in second position (6 blow as the tonic).

GAROUN

Armenia

50

4 4 4 5   6 6 ⑤   ④ 4 ③ 4   ④ 5 ④ 4

"Garoun" is a popular Armenian folk song whose title means "Springtime".

BINT EL SHALABIYA

Lebanon(?)

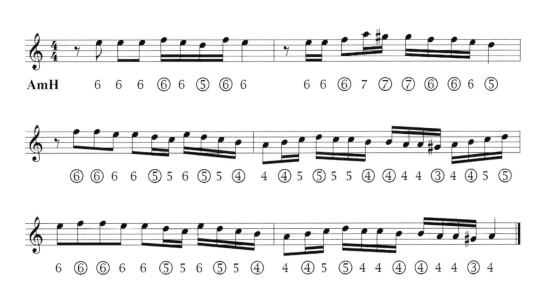

AmH   6   6   6 ⑥ 6 ⑤ ⑥ 6   6 6 ⑥ 7 ⑦ ⑦ ⑥ ⑥ 6 ⑤

⑥ ⑥ 6 6 ⑤ 5 6 ⑤ 5 ④   4 ④ 5 ⑤ 5 5 ④ ④ 4 4 ③ 4 ④ 5 ⑤

6 ⑥ ⑥ 6 6 ⑤ 5 6 ⑤ 5 ④   4 ④ 5 ⑤ 4 4 ④ ④ 4 4 ③ 4

There is some dispute over the origins of this tune, whose Arabic title means "The Beautiful Girl". Lyrics to it exist in Arabic, Farsi, Turkish and Hebrew.

CAPTAIN KIDD

England

Captain William Kidd was a notorious Scottish sailor who was executed for piracy (many believe unjustly) in 1701. There are many different versions of the tune, in both major keys and minor keys, as well as modal versions - this one is very firmly in the harmonic minor. There are also many different lyrics, telling of the legendary Captain's exploits with varying degrees of accuracy.

KOLOMEYKES

Ukraine

A traditional Ukrainian dance tune. The first part is straight harmonic minor, the second part shifts to the fourth mode of the harmonic minor scale.

ODESSA BULGAR

Klezmer

A famous klezmer dance tune in the fourth mode of the harmonic minor, played in 12th position (5 draw as the tonic).

POLTAVS'KIY

Ukraine

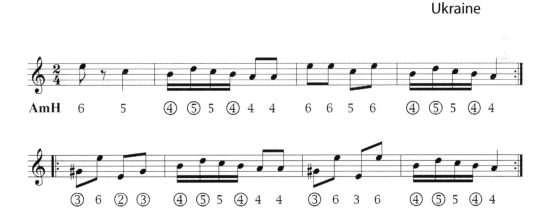

A somewhat less famous dance tune of Ukrainian origin.

MINUET

Robert de Visée

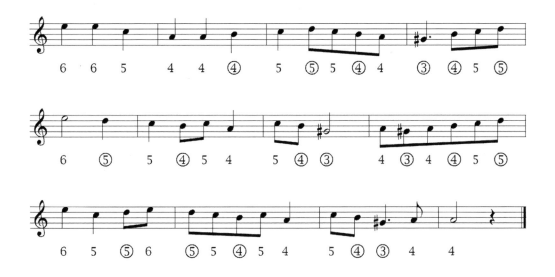

Robert de Visée (1655 – 1733) was a composer who sang and played lute, guitar, viol and theorbo at the court of Louis XIV of France. Little is known about him - he may have been Portuguese by birth and even his dates of birth and death are not certain. However, he was a prolific and highly influential composer for the guitar.

The minuet (or menuet) was a very popular social dance in 17th and 18th century Europe, probably originating in Italy. This particular example was originally written in Dm.

OLÁHOS

Hungary

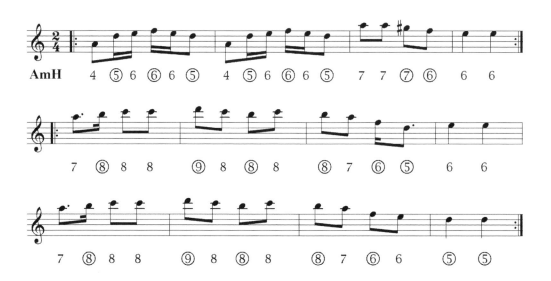

METELYTSYA

Ukraine

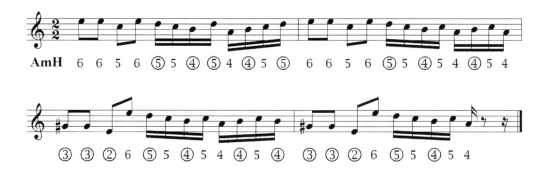

Two East European dance tunes. "Oláhos" is from Southern Hungary and is in the fourth mode of the harmonic minor scale. "Metelytsya" is of Ukrainian origin and is straight harmonic minor.

POVRATENO

Macedonia

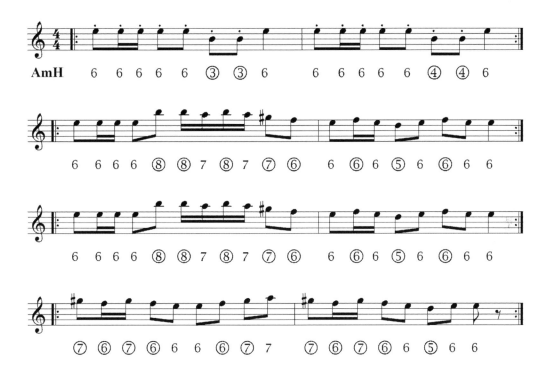

A line dance tune from Central Macedonia, originally danced by men only.

HORAH HEMED

Israel

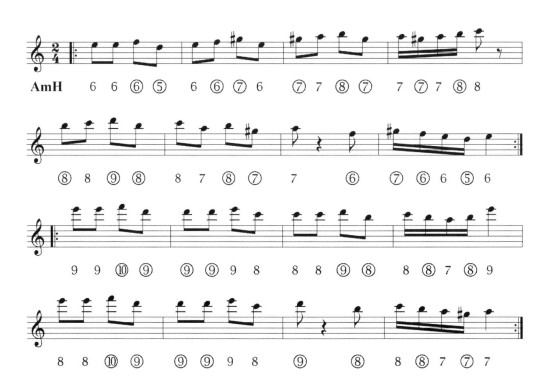

The *horah*, also known as *hora, oro* and *xopo*, is a circle dance popular in the Balkans and neighbouring countries, as well as amongst Gypsy and klezmer musicians.

"Hora Ca Din Caval" accompanies a Romanian version of this dance, the *caval* being a flute played by shepherds. This tune is in the fourth mode of the harmonic minor and varies quite a lot between different performers, some versions almost having a jazz swing feel to them. The most famous recording of it was by pan flute artist Gheorghe Zamfir.

HORA CA DIN CAVAL

Romania

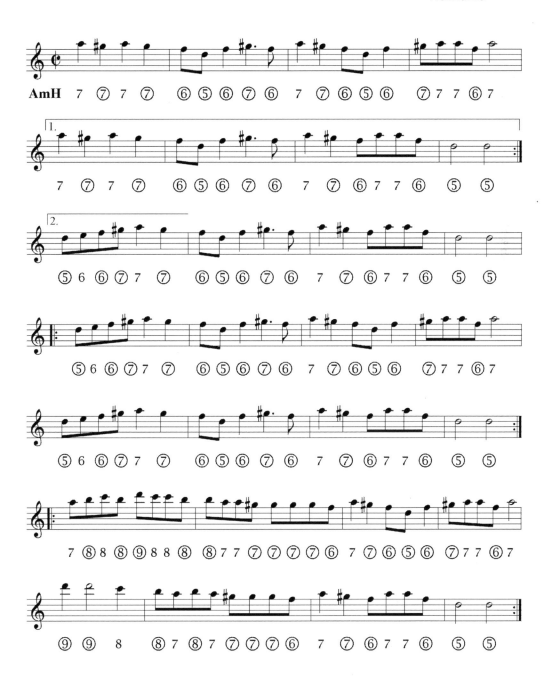

LA LIAUDE

France

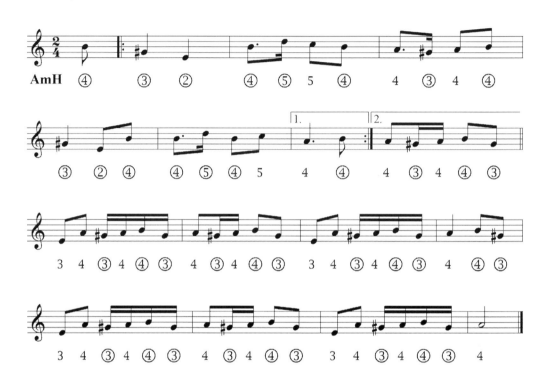

A bourrée from Central France. The A section may feel a little odd, as it is six bars long, unlike the more conventional eight bar B section.

SIMONS PERS VALS

Sweden

A waltz tune from Dalarna Cunty, Sweden.

OZHIDANIE

Russia

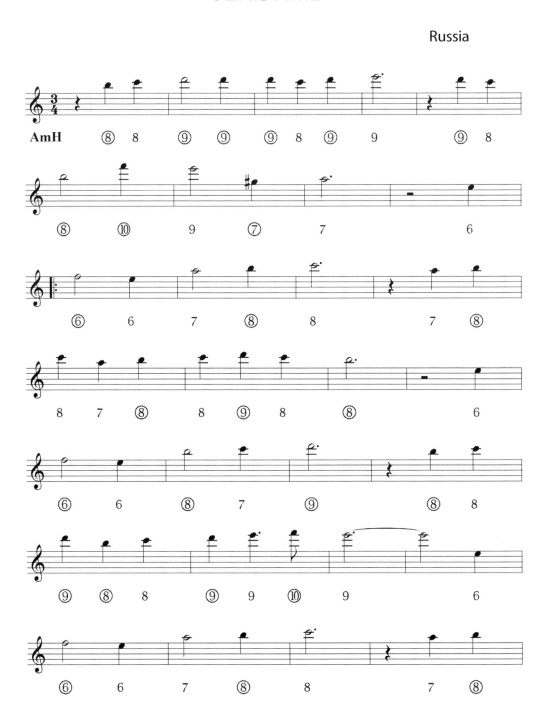

64

Yet another waltz, this time from Russia. The title means "Expectation" and it is commonly sung with Yiddish lyrics as "Mayn Ershter Vals" or "My First Waltz".

LA ROSINA NEL ROSAL

Spain (Asturias)

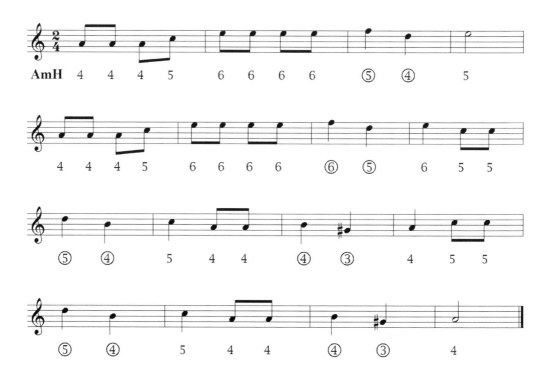

Another beautiful melody from the Principality of Asturias in Northern Spain, where the harmonic minor scale seems to be very popular in the local folk music.

LJUGAREN

Sweden

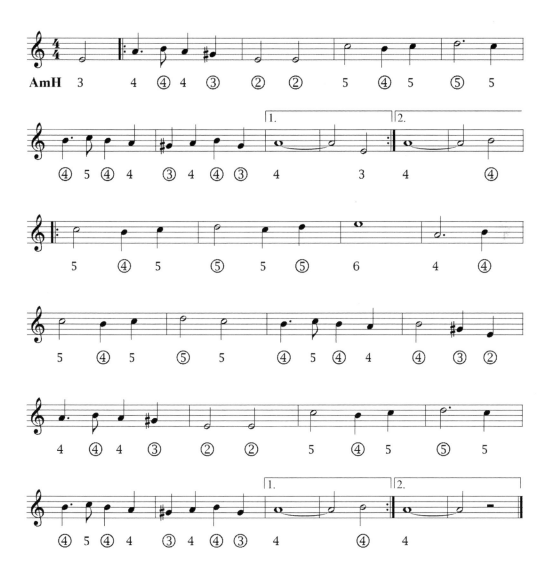

Another tune associated with the Swedish bagpipes, this one is from Dalarna along the border between Sweden and Norway.

SI J'AVAIS UN BON AMI

France

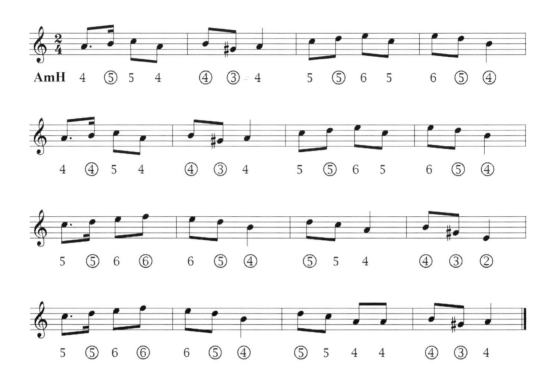

AmH 4 ⑤ 5 4 ④ ③ 4 5 ⑤ 6 5 6 ⑤ ④

4 ④ 5 4 ④ ③ 4 5 ⑤ 6 5 6 ⑤ ④

5 ⑤ 6 ⑥ 6 ⑤ ④ ⑤ 5 4 ④ ③ ②

5 ⑤ 6 ⑥ 6 ⑤ ④ ⑤ 5 4 4 ④ ③ 4

Two bourrées from the folk tradition of Central France. Somewhat similar to the gavotte, the bourrée also became very popular with classical composers such as Bach, Chopin and Handel.

The first tune also has lyrics and the title translates as "If I Had A Good Friend". The second one translates as "Do You Know Why?" I don't know why and I don't know whether there are lyrics to this one or not.

SAVEZ-VOUS POURQUOI?

France

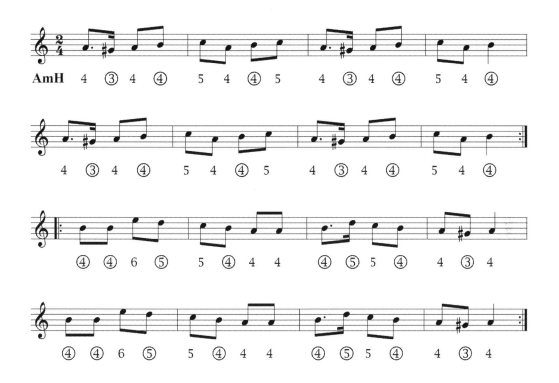

69

GÅNGLÅT

Sweden

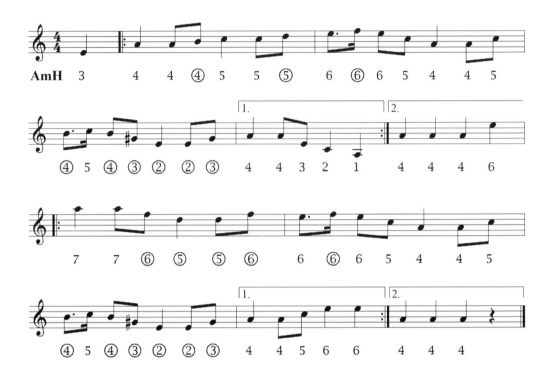

Yet another folk dance form from Sweden, the gånglåt comes from the fiddle tradition, rather than from the Swedish bagpipes. The majority of them seem to be untitled.

GÅNGLÅT FRÅN PITEÅ

Sweden

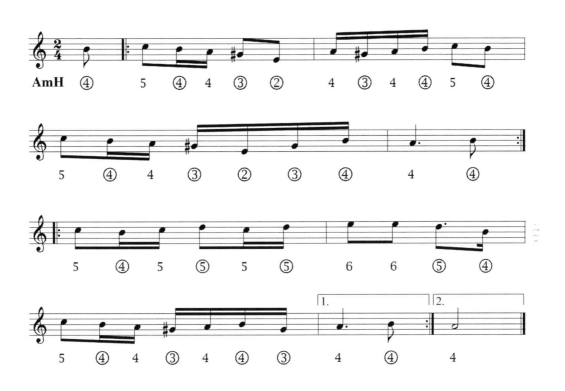

Another gånglåt. At least we know that this one comes from Piteå, in Northern Sweden.

POLONÄS FRÅN SEXDREGA

Sweden

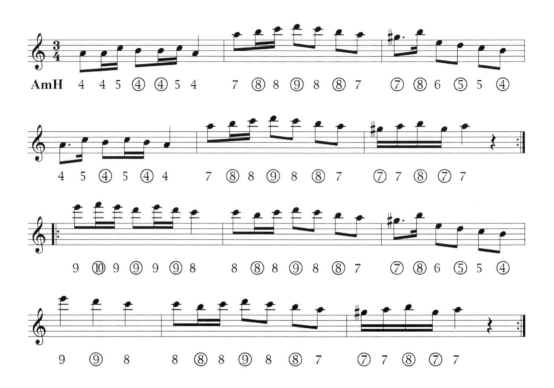

Yet another dance form popular in traditional Swedish dance music, the polonaise originated in Poland - in fact the name polonaise is French for Polish.

PRINCIPESSA

Italy

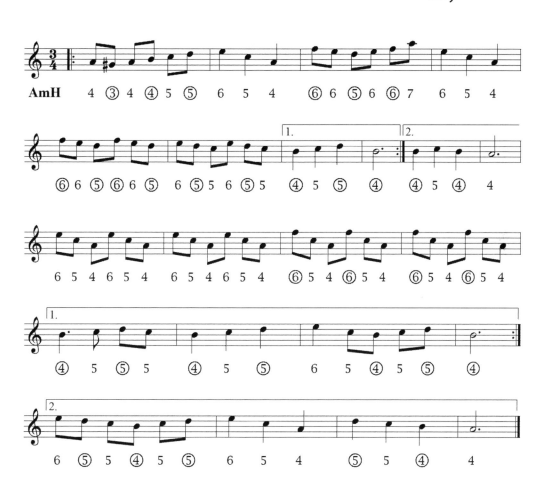

The mazurka is another dance of Polish origin, which became popular with composers such as Chopin, Tchaikovsky, Debussy and Ravel. This particular example comes from the Piedmont region of Northern Italy

THE MILLER OF DEE

England

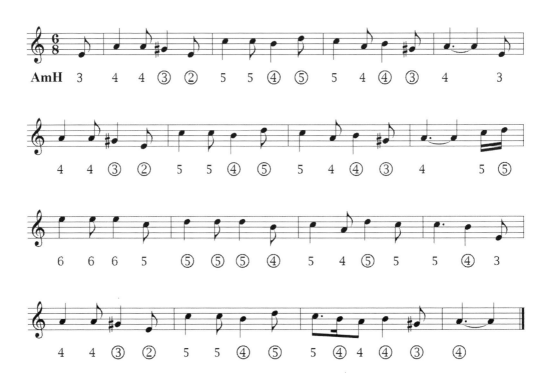

When I gathered together the tunes for this book, I was surprised at how many traditional English songs used the harmonic minor scale. Here are a couple more.

"The Miller of Dee" comes from Northwest England near the border with Wales and possibly borrows its melody from an older Welsh tune. It has orchestral settings by Benjamin Britten and Ludwig Van Beethoven, amongst others.

74

HOW UNHAPPY IS PHYLLIS IN LOVE

England

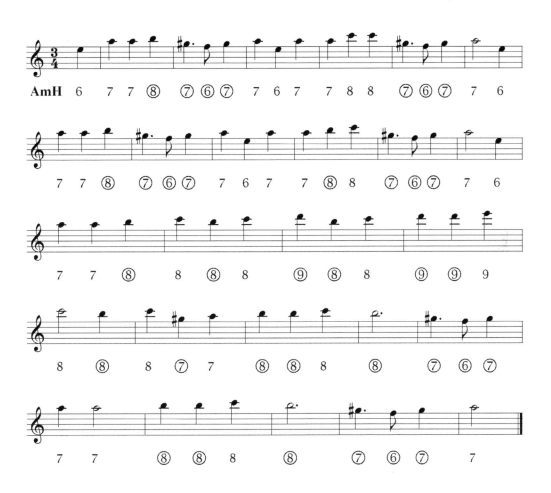

An English ballad with some rather un-English sounding phrases in it, dating back to some time around the late 17th century.

ILLAN HILJAISUUDESSA

Finland

76

A Finnish folk song whose title translates as "In the Still of the Evening".

SERRAS DREJELIREN

Denmark

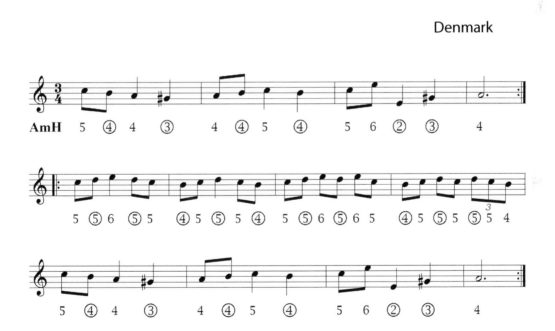

A dance tune from Rasmus Storm's Notebook, a handwritten collection of tunes compiled by a Danish fiddler of the 19th century.

CANTICO

Venezuela

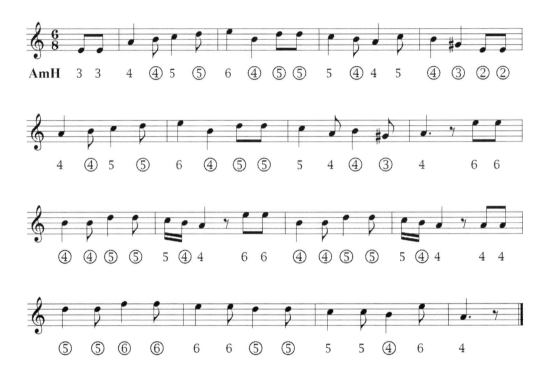

A traditional Venezuelan tune, made popular by an arrangement for the guitar by Vicente Emilio Sojo.

TUNES WITH BENDS

SPANISH LADIES

England

Let's start off this section with a tune that only requires one bend - a two semitone bend on 3 draw, to give an ascending melodic minor scale.

"Spanish Ladies" is a well-known naval song, dating at least as far back as the 18th century. As is typical of these types of songs, there are many different sets of lyrics and quite a few different versions of the melody, although most versions begin with the lines "Farewell and adieu to you, Spanish Ladies".

VEM KAN SEGLA FÖRUTAN VIND?

Sweden/Finland

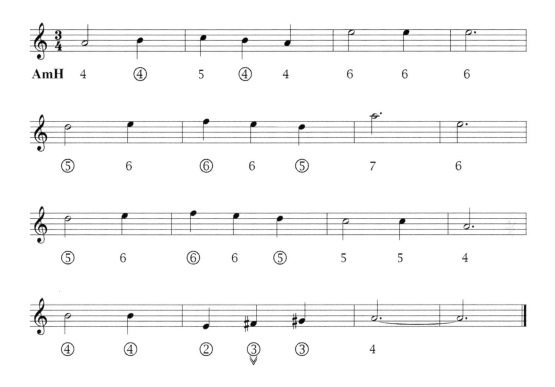

A haunting ballad whose title means "Who Can Sail Without The Wind?", this tune comes from the Åland Islands in the Baltic Sea. At various points in history, these islands have been considered a part of Sweden, but they are currently an autonomous region of Finland, although the inhabitants all speak Swedish.

This tune has many different settings, some in waltz time like this one, some in 6/8 and others in 4/4 time. The melody given here is slightly different from the most common version and sits nicely on a harmonic minor harp, with just a single two semitone bend on 3 draw.

NIGUN ATIK

Israel

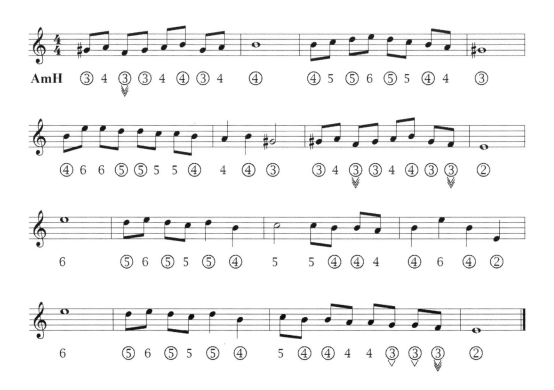

This tune is in the fifth mode of the harmonic minor scale, played in second position, leaning heavily on the three semitone bend on 3 draw. Look out for the G naturals in the last bar, played with single semitone bends on 3 draw.

The title means simply "Old Tune" and it is commonly played for wedding dances.

SVARTERABBEN

Norway

AmH 4 ④ 5 ⑤ 6 ⑥ 6 ⑤ ④ ⑤ 5   ④ 4 ③ 4 ④ 5 4 ③ ②

4 5 ⑤ 6 ⑥ 6 ⑤ ④ ⑤ 5   ④ 4 ③ 4 ④ 5 4 ③ 4

6 ② ② ② ② ② ② ② ②   6 ② ② ② ② ② ② ② ②

4 5 ⑤ 6 ⑥ 6 ⑤ ⑥   7 7 7 7 7 7 7

A folk song featured in the 1939 film "Gjest Baardsen", the story of a notorious 19th century Norwegian outlaw. This arrangement requires a couple of bent notes, both of them two semitone bends on 2 draw. It could also be played an octave higher without any bends needed.

MISIRLOU

Greece

AmH   6 ⑥ ⑦ 7   ⑧ 8 9 8   ⑧
                                  ∧

6 ⑥ ⑦ 7   ⑧ 8 9 8   ⑧
                        ∧

8 ⑧ 8 ⑧ 7   ⑧ 7 ⑧ 7   ⑦   ⑦

⑧ 7 ⑧ 7 ⑦   ⑦ 6 ⑦ 6 6   6

7   ⑦ 7 ⑧   7 ⑧ 8 ⑧ 8   9 8 9 9
                                  ∧   ∧

⑩ 9 ⑩ 9   ⑨   9 ⑨ 9 ⑨ 8   ⑧

⑨ 8 ⑨ 8 ⑧   ⑧ 7 ⑧ ⑦ ⑥   6

84

This tune became extremely well known after Dick Dale's surf guitar version of it was featured in the movie "Pulp Fiction". There is some dispute as to the song's origins, but it was first recorded in Greece by rebetiko artist Michalis Patrinos.

This arrangement is in second position on the harmonic minor harp. The first section uses the *hitzazkiar* scale (E F G# A B C D# E) and requires a one semitone blow bend on blow 9 to play the D#. The second part of the tune uses a D natural and requires no bends.

VALS

Norway

An untitled Norwegian waltz, this also requires a one semitone bend on hole 9, but to rather different effect from the previous tune.

TSAMIKOS

Greece

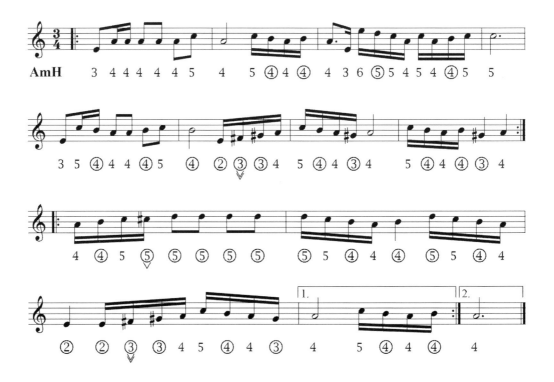

Tsamikos is a slow Greek dance in 3/4 time. Traditionally, it was danced only by men, but now both men and women dance it. This arrangement has a couple of two semitone bends on 3 draw and a single semitone bend on 5 draw.

BRUDMARSCH FRÅN DALBY

Sweden

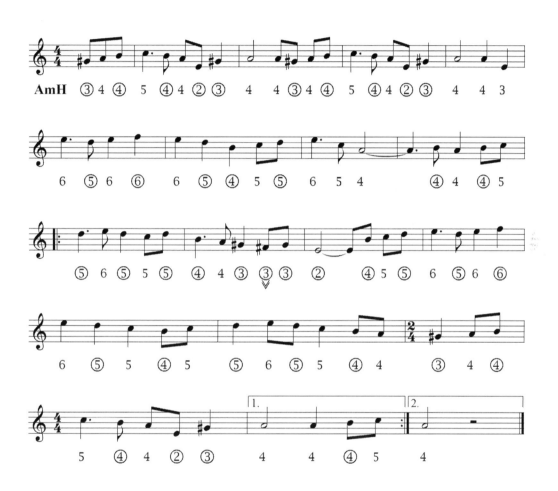

This bridal march from Dalby in Southern Sweden has a single two semitone bend on 3 draw.

ROUND DANCE

Russia

This tune uses both the descending and the ascending forms of the melodic minor scale. Bar 12 has a G natural (one semitone band on 3 draw) and an F natural (three semitone bend on 3 draw). Bar 16 has an F# (two semitone bend on 3 draw) and a G# (3 draw unbent). It may be worth practising along with a keyboard or an electronic tuner to make sure that you are getting each of these bends accurately.

BOURRÉE

Robert de Visée

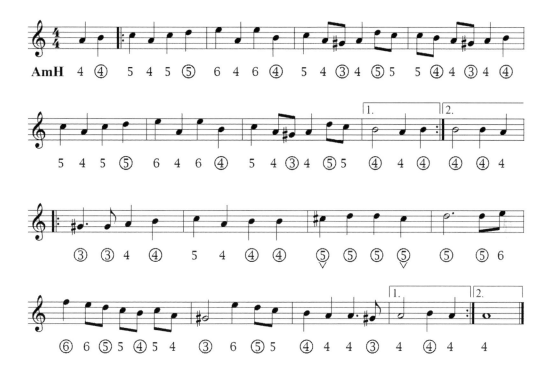

A second piece by Robert de Visée. Like his "Minuet" (see page 56), this was also originally written in Dm. This piece requires a couple of one semitone bends on 5 draw.

ARABER TANZ

Klezmer

A piece from the klezmer tradition whose title means "Arab Dance". The tune is in the fifth mode of the harmonic minor, arranged here for second position in the upper octave and requiring a single one semitone bend on blow 9.

AH YA ZAIN

Syria

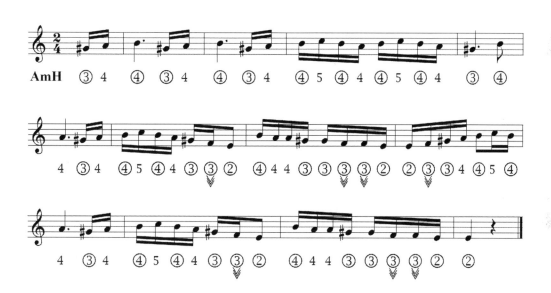

Most likely of Syrian origin, this tune is often played for belly dancers. This arrangement is in second position in the lowest octave of the harmonic minor harp and leans heavily on the three semitone bend on draw 3.

CADE L'ULIVA

Italy

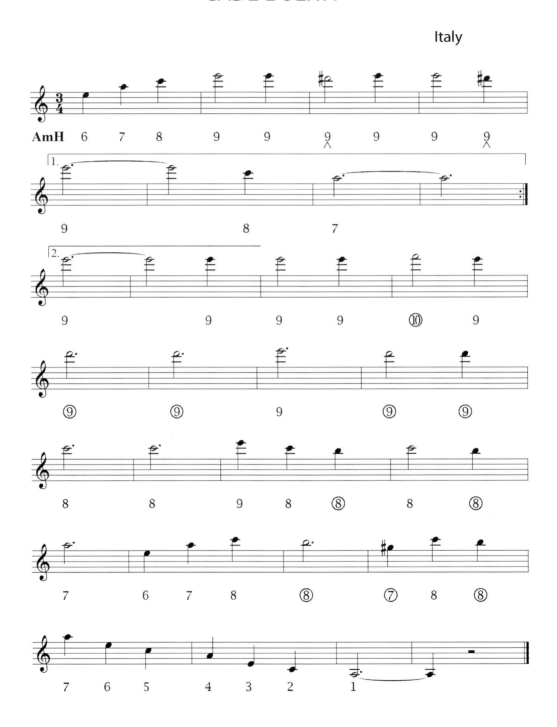

A haunting love song from Central Italy, whose title means "The Olive Falls".
The opening part of the melody leans heavily on the raised fourth note of the
harmonic minor scale, which makes it sound almost Middle Eastern, rather
than European.

CRIMSON VELVET

England

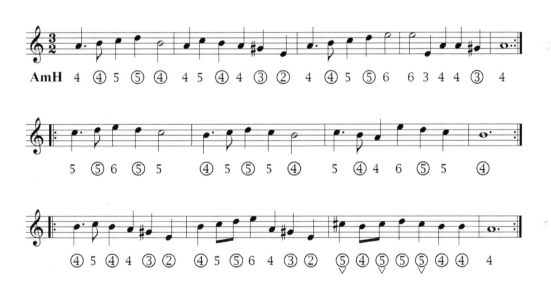

Dating back to the early 17th century, this is another melody that has been
used for several different songs. The tune is quite straightforward until the last
two bars, where it moves to the parallel major key. This requires a one semitone bend on 5 draw, but it might take some work to get it to sound clean and
smooth.

VALSE

France

An untitled waltz from France, requiring a single two semitone bend on 3 draw.

VALS

Norway

Another untitled waltz tune, this time from Norway, requiring a two semitone bend on 2 draw.

VALS FRÅN VÄRMLAND

Sweden

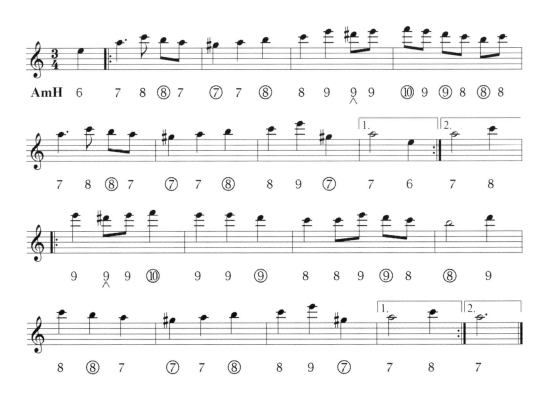

One last untitled waltz, this time from Värmland in Western Sweden and requiring a couple of one semitone bends on 9 blow.

DRAGAICUTA

Romania

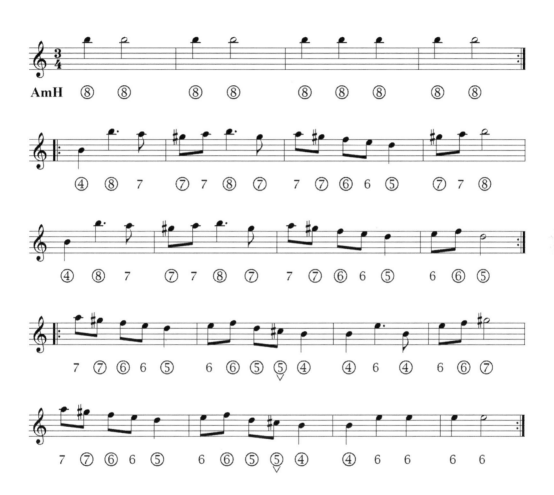

Another tune in 3/4 time, but this time not a waltz! "Draigacuta" is Romanian folk dance with agricultural associations. Arranged here for second position on an AmH harp, the scale used for this tune is an interesting one - E F G# A B C# D E - the C# being played by bending 5 draw.

DANTZ

Denmark

A couple more tunes from Rasmus Storm's Notebook. The succinctly titled "Dantz" ("Dance") requires a two semitone bend on 2 draw, whilst "Fransk Morgenstierne" ("French Morning Star") requires the obligatory two semitone bend on 3 draw.

FRANSK MORGENSTIERNE

Denmark

HORA FETELOR

Romania

4 ③ ③ 4 ④ 4 ③ ③ 4 ③ ③ ③ ② ② ②

"Hora Fetelor" is another Romanian tune with an unusual scale, this time the fifth mode of the melodic minor scale - E F# G A B C D E (see page 17) - with a low D# added. It requires good clean two semitone bends on 3 draw, as well as single semitone bends on 2 draw.

VE DAVID

Israel

AmH ② ④ ④ 5 ④ 5 ④ 4   ③ 4 ③ ③ ② ② ②

② 4 4 4 ④ 4 ④   ② ④ ④ ⑤ 5 ④ 4 ④

③ ③ ③ 4 ③ ③ ②   ④ ④ ④ 5 ④ 4 ④
                     ③ ③ ③ 4 ③ 3 ③
                                        ②

A traditional Israeli dance tune in the fifth mode of the harmonic minor scale, with a few double stops thrown in to fill out the sound a little.

KIVELE

Yiddish

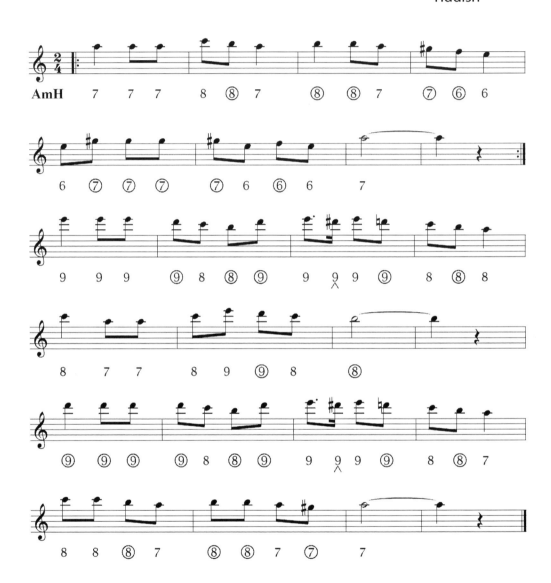

A traditional Yiddish lullaby, a popular recording of it was made in the 1920s by Max Reichart.

RIGODOON

England

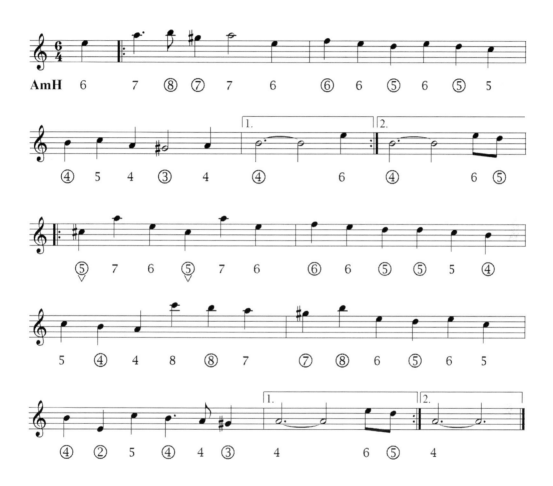

A tune from Lancashire, England. Like "Crimson Velvet" (see page 93), it borrows from the parallel major key in the second section, requiring some clean bending technique on 5 draw.

AMBEE DAGEETS

Armenia

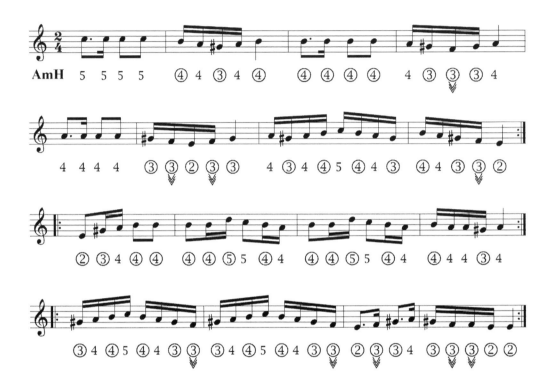

Also known as "Ambi Dagits" or "Armenian Turns", this is a line dancing tune set in the fifth mode of the harmonic minor scale. I think it sounds good in the lower octave of the harmonica, with heavy use of the three semitone bend on 3 draw, although it can also be played an octave higher without bends.

YOSHKE FORT AVEK

Klezmer

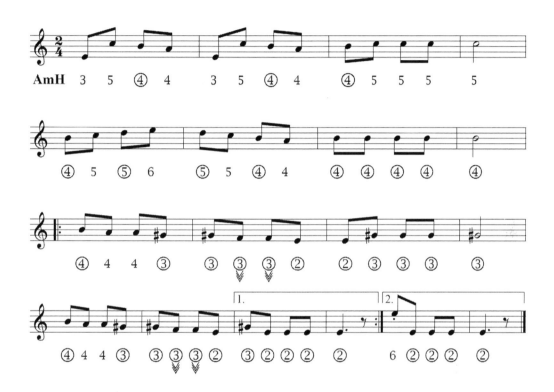

"Yoshke Is Leaving", a klezmer tune closely related to the Smyrnaic tune "Mangiko". Again, set in the fifth mode of the harmonic minor scale and played in low octave second position with lots of three semitone 3 draw bends.

THE SILVER WEDDING

Klezmer

A couple more klezmer tunes, both of them freilachs, both of them in the fifth mode of the harmonic minor, both of them played in low octave second position and both of them leaning on the three semitone bend on 3 draw. Both of them good tunes, too!

DAN'S FREILACH

Klezmer

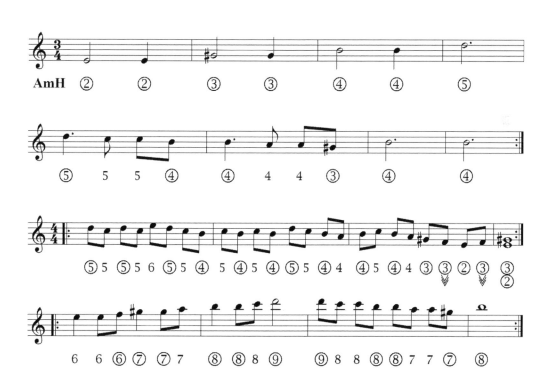

GIVE ME A ROSE

China

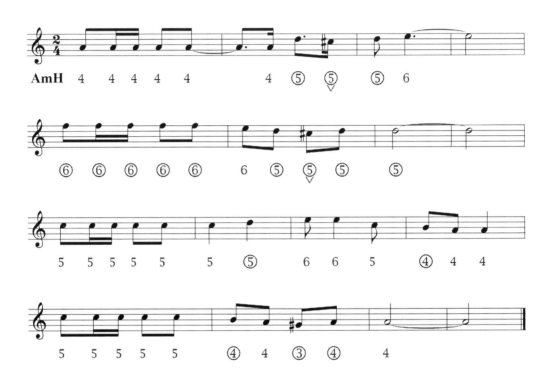

A song from the Uyghur minority of Northwest China. Its unusual melodic lines require a couple of bends on 5 draw.

108

BOURRÉE DU BERRY

France

A bourrée in 3/8 time from the Auvergne region of Central France.

ET DODIM KALA

Israel

A couple of traditional Israeli dance tunes, both in the fifth mode of the harmonic minor and arranged for low octave second position. "Et Dodim Kala" means "Song of Songs" and "Nitzotz Ha'ahava" means "The Spark of Love".

NITZOTZ HA AHAVA

Israel

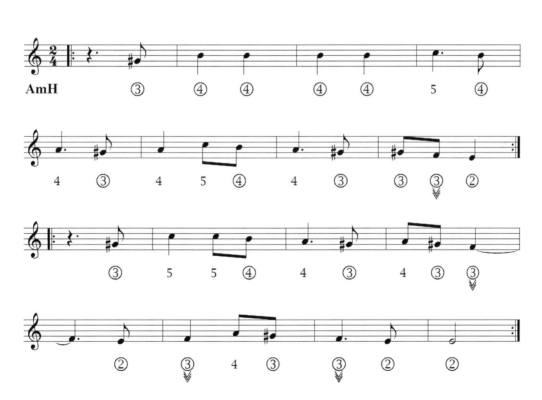

SCHOTTIS FRÅN HAVERÖ

Sweden

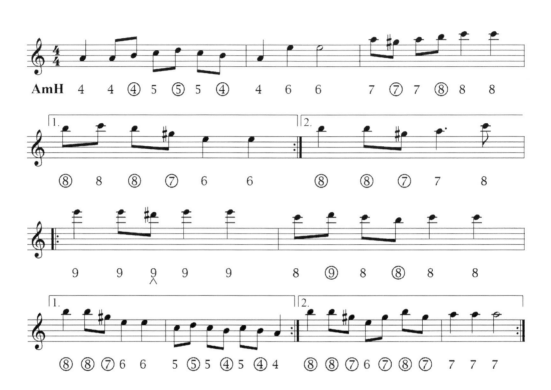

Despite its name, the schottische seems to have originated in Bohemia, rather than in Scotland. The Swedish version seems closely related to the Norwegian Reinlender. This one from Häverö in Central Sweden requires a single bend on 9 blow.

TALGOXEN

Finland

AmH   6 7 7 6 5 4   ④5 ④ ③ ② ②   ② ③ ③ ④ ④ ② ③ ④   4 ④5 ⑤6 6

6 7 7 6 5   4   ④5 ④ ③ ② ②   ② ③ ③ ④ ④ ② ③ ④   4   4   4

⑥ ⑥ ⑤ ⑥ ⑥ ⑤   6 6 5 6 6 5   ⑤ ⑤ ④ ⑤ ⑤ ④   5 ④5 ⑤6 6

⑥ ⑥ ⑤ ⑥ ⑥ ⑤   6 6 5 6 6 5   ⑤5 ④4 ③ ② ③ ③   4   4   4

The title of this polka from Finland is the local name for the songbird *Parus Major* and some of the phrases seem almost to imitate the call of this bird. Just a single bend needed - a two semitone band on 3 draw.

113

CERDETSHNI

Russia

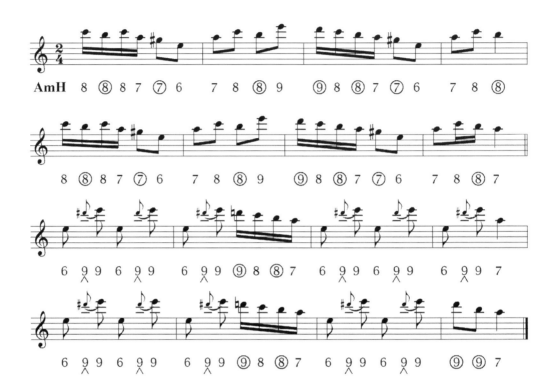

A Russian tune popular with balalaika players, the 9 blow bends are used as grace notes to slide into the unbent 9 blow notes.

NORITS KAROON YEGAV

Armenia

An Armenian tune to finish off this chapter. A popular tune for belly dancing, arranged here for low octave second position, with bends on 5 draw and those deep three semitone bends on draw 3.

ABOUT THE NOTATION USED IN THIS BOOK

Tablature, often abbreviated to tab, is a notational system that instead of representing the notes themselves, represents where these notes are to be found on the instrument in question.

Tablature has a long history, being used during the Renaissance for such instruments as lute and vihuela. Tab became very popular in the 20th century with "folk instruments" such as guitar, banjo, harmonica, etc., for the simple reason that it enables someone to work out how to play a tune without having to learn to read standard musical notation. However, I believe that by itself, tab is extremely limited and for that reason, all the tunes and musical examples in this book are notated in both standard notation and tab - the standard notation tells you what notes are to be played and what rhythmic values they should be given, the tab shows how these notes are to be played on the harmonica.

There have been many forms of harmonica tablature devised over the years. The system I use in this book is SuperTab, created by Steve Jennings. The essentials of the system are quite straightforward.

A plain number indicates to blow into the hole that bears that number. A circled number indicates to draw into that hole. For example, this shows a the Am harmonic minor scale played in the middle octave of a harmonic minor harp in AmH:

Chords and double stops are indicated by numbers above one another. This example shows an E chord played in holes 2, 3 and 4 draw of an AmH harp, followed by an Am major chord played in holes 3, 4 and 5 blow:

An arrowhead underneath a number indicates a bent note, the number of arrowheads indicates the number of semitones the note should be bent. Additionally, the direction of the arrowhead corresponds to the breath direction, pointing upwards for blow notes and downwards for draw notes. This example shows 2 draw bent by two semitones, 2 draw played unbent, 3 draw bent by one semitone, two draw played unbent, 1 draw played unbent, then 1 draw bent by a semitone:

This example shows 9 blow bent by a semitone, 9 draw played unbent, 10 blow played unbent, then 10 blow bent by two semitones:

An upwards pointing arrowhead above a number indicates an overblow and a downwards pointing arrowhead above a circled number indicates an overdraw. However, these techniques are not used in any of the tunes in this book.

I have followed my usual practice of notating everything with the key signature of the harmonica used to play the tune, regardless of the key of the tune itself. As all the tunes and musical examples in this book are given as played on an AmH harp, that means everything is written with the key signature of C major/A minor.

NOTE LAYOUT CHARTS

Here are the note layouts for each of the twelve keys of harmonic minor harp, from GmH (usually the lowest key) to F#mH (usually the highest key).

	1	2	3	4	5	6	7	8	9	10	
	G	B♭	D	G	B♭	D	G	B♭	D	G	
Gm	1	2	3	4	5	6	7	8	9	10	**H**
	A	D	F#	A	C	E♭	F#	A	C	E♭	

	A♭	C♭	E♭	A♭	C♭	E♭	A♭	C♭	E♭	A♭	
A♭m	1	2	3	4	5	6	7	8	9	10	**H**
	B♭	E♭	G	B♭	D♭	F♭	G	B♭	D♭	F♭	

	A	C	E	A	C	E	A	C	E	A	
Am	1	2	3	4	5	6	7	8	9	10	**H**
	B	E	G#	B	D	F	G#	B	D	F	

B♭m	B♭	D♭	F	B♭	D♭	F	B♭	D♭	F	B♭	H
	1	2	3	4	5	6	7	8	9	10	
	C	F	A	C	E♭	G♭	A	C	E♭	G♭	

Bm	B	D	F#	B	D	F#	B	D	F#	B	H
	1	2	3	4	5	6	7	8	9	10	
	C#	F#	A#	C#	E	G	A#	C#	E	G	

Cm	C	E♭	G	C	E♭	G	C	E♭	G	C	H
	1	2	3	4	5	6	7	8	9	10	
	D	G	B	D	F	A♭	B	D	F	A♭	

	Db	Fb	Ab	Db	Fb	Ab	Db	Fb	Ab	Db	
Dbm	1	2	3	4	5	6	7	8	9	10	**H**
	Eb	Ab	C	Eb	Gb	Bbb	C	Eb	Gb	Bbb	

	D	F	A	D	F	A	D	F	A	D	
Dm	1	2	3	4	5	6	7	8	9	10	**H**
	E	A	C#	E	G	Bb	C#	E	G	Bb	

	Eb	Gb	Bb	Eb	Gb	Bb	Eb	Gb	Bb	Eb	
Ebm	1	2	3	4	5	6	7	8	9	10	**H**
	F	Bb	D	F	Ab	Cb	D	F	Ab	Cb	

E	G	B	E	G	B	E	G	B	E
Em 1	2	3	4	5	6	7	8	9	10 **H**
F#	B	D#	F#	A	C	D#	F#	A	C

F	A♭	C	F	A♭	C	F	A♭	C	F
Fm 1	2	3	4	5	6	7	8	9	10 **H**
G	C	E	G	B♭	D♭	E	G	B♭	D♭

F#	A	C#	F#	A	C#	F#	A	C#	F#
F#m 1	2	3	4	5	6	7	8	9	10 **H**
G#	C#	E#	G#	B	D	E#	G#	B	D

121

INDEX TO THE TUNES

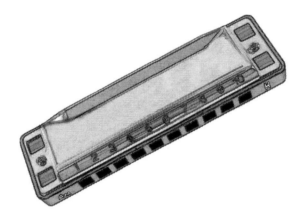

IF YOU ENJOYED THIS BOOK...

... check out this one:

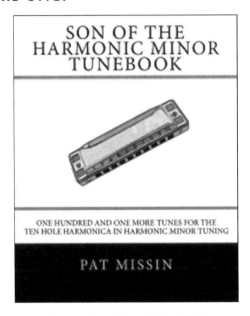

SON OF THE HARMONIC MINOR TUNEBOOK

ONE HUNDRED AND ONE MORE TUNES FOR THE TEN HOLE HARMONICA IN HARMONIC MINOR TUNING

A companion volume to *The Harmonic Minor Tunebook*, containing more than a hundred tunes arranged for the harmonic minor tuned harmonica.

Included are traditional tunes from all over the world, plus selections from classical composers such as Saint-Saëns, Schumann and Carcassi, presented in both standard notation and tablature.

Also included are useful tips on playing blues and jazz on the harmonic minor harp, playing in unfamilar time signatures, playing harmonic minor tremolo harps, using multiple harmonicas on a single tune and the harmonic minor tuning compared with the natural minor tuning.

.mp3 files of all the tunes in the book are available for free download from the author's web site.

BY THE SAME AUTHOR

HOW TO PLAY BAWU AND HULUSI

A BEGINNER'S GUIDE TO THESE POPULAR CHINESE WIND INSTRUMENTS

THE BAWU AND HULUSI TUNEBOOK

ONE HUNDRED AND ONE TUNES FOR THESE POPULAR CHINESE WIND INSTRUMENTS

WESTERN TUNES FOR BAWU AND HULUSI

ONE HUNDRED AND ONE NON-CHINESE TUNES FOR THESE POPULAR CHINESE WIND INSTRUMENTS

CHRISTMAS TUNES FOR BAWU AND HULUSI

125 SEASONAL FAVORITES FOR THESE POPULAR CHINESE WIND INSTRUMENTS

THE ULTIMATE MINIATURE HARMONICA TUNEBOOK

365 TUNES FOR THE FOUR HOLE HARMONICA

NOTES

NOTES

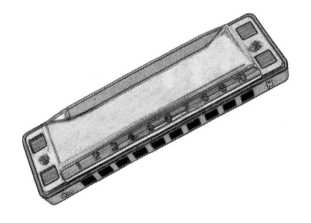

www.patmissin.com

Printed in Great Britain
by Amazon